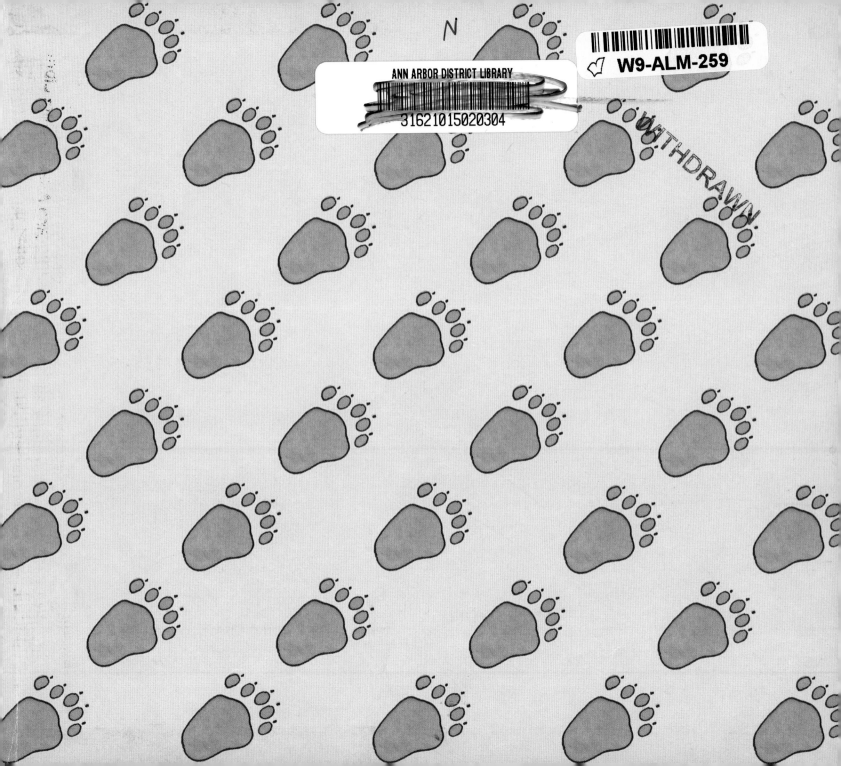

W9-ALM-259

Backyard Bear

by Anne Rockwell   pictures by Megan Halsey

WALKER & COMPANY
New York

One winter day, a bear came to a cave in the woods.
She squeezed and wriggled inside,
then lay down to sleep.
While snow fell outside,
the bear gave birth to a tiny cub.
He nursed from the mother bear,
and she slept on, her thick fur keeping him warm.

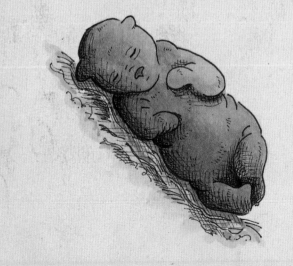

When spring came,

the mother bear and her cub came out of the cave.

He was bigger and furrier now.

His mother showed him how to dig for roots and grubs to eat.

Summer came, and berries ripened. Bees made honey.

Sometimes the bears found birds' eggs alone in a nest,

which were very special treats.

If the cub strayed too far from his mother,

she gave him scolding grunts.

She taught him to climb trees quickly to escape danger
and to sleep comfortably on branches.
Every day she and her cub played together:
chasing, play fighting, and rolling down hills.
She licked his fur to keep him clean.
The mother bear taught her cub
many things he needed to know.

As he and his mother hunted for food in the summer woods,
the cub ate and ate and grew bigger and fatter.
In the fall, ripe nuts and acorns fell to the ground.
When winter came, the bears returned to their warm cave,
where they snuggled up and went to sleep again.

The next spring, when they came out of the cave,
things had changed in their woods.
Chainsaws were cutting down trees.
Bulldozers and backhoes were pushing earth around.
Hammers pounded, and saws buzzed.
The bears were scared of the strange, loud noises,
so they hid.

One morning, the cub's mother wouldn't play with him.

Instead she grunted fiercely and cuffed his nose.

The cub didn't understand,

but his mother knew it was time

for him to take care of himself.

She ran off and left him alone.

He cried for his mother,
but there was no answer.
Instead there was a loud shout from workers
as a tall tree crashed to the forest floor—
a tree the cub and his mother liked to climb.

A doe and two fawns leaped out of the underbrush
and ran away. They were scared when the tree fell down.
The cub ran up another tree and went on crying and crying,
but his mother didn't come back.
That's the way it is when bear cubs get big.

Soon people came to live in the brand-new houses
the workers built.
At first the bear cub was scared of them,
but then he discovered that their yards had good things to eat.
The bear cub stopped searching for food in the forest.
The green grassy backyards had all the food he needed.

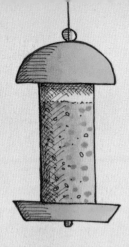

There were bird feeders full of seed.
Sometimes there were scraps under picnic tables,
or dog bones and bowls of water on back stoops.
Of course, that meant there were also dogs
that lived in the houses,
but the young bear ran up a tree if they were around.
Best of all, there were garbage cans full of delicious things.

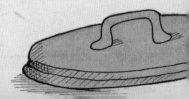

On a sunny autumn afternoon a mother was out
in her backyard with her baby boy
who was just learning to walk and talk.
The bear was eating an apple
that fell from a tree at the end of the yard.
"Bah!" said the baby boy,
for that was what he called his teddy bear.
As soon as the mother saw the bear, she screamed,
picked up her baby, and ran indoors.
The bear was scared of the loud noise
and ran into the bushes.

The dog from next door ran barking after him,
so the bear hurried up a nearby pine tree.
While the bear was in the tree,
the baby's mother telephoned
the state game warden
to say there was a bear in her yard.
He told her the bear had to be moved.
It wasn't safe around people and dogs,
paved roads, and cars.

Two game wardens drove up in a truck
with a wire cage in the back.
They set the cage on the grass,
covered the floor with marshmallows,
and opened the door.
One warden put a leash on the dog
and walked it home.
The other warden hid very quietly
behind the family's tall tomato plants.
Then the first warden returned and hid, too.
After a few minutes,
the bear came down
and sniffed the marshmallows.

As soon as the bear was inside eating marshmallows,
one game warden shut the door of the cage.
He gave the bear a shot.
Before he had eaten all the marshmallows,
the bear fell asleep.
The wardens put the cage onto their truck.
They drove the bear far away from the new houses
to a place where bears could roam.

The bear's new home was full of nuts and acorns.
It even had a small cave where the bear
could curl up and sleep for the long winter.
No people lived there, so it was a good place for him—
a safe place in the wild woods where he belonged.
His new home was where he could grow up
to be a big, wild bear.

Author's Note

The bear in this story is a black bear, which is found in most wooded parts of the United States and Canada. Black bears are smaller and less aggressive than the larger grizzly bears, whose habitat is the far West of the United States and Canada. Black bears are usually shy, but as humans move into their habitats, there is a danger that they'll become dependent upon garbage and other food found in backyards. It is possible they will become aggressive over their food supply, becoming a dangerous problem for people and pets.

Bears have been seen in suburban streets, malls, and backyards as people build more and more developments in what has been the bears' habitat. In my own densely populated state of Connecticut, there were 1,300 bear sightings in the past year.

There are things we can do to keep bears away. We can use bird feeders only in winter when bears are asleep, or hang them at least twelve feet above ground. We can clean up any fruit that falls to the ground, keep our garbage in bear-proof containers, and lock up outdoor cooking grills in garages or sheds when not in use. By doing these things, our yards will become less tempting to bears, making them search for food in the woods, as they are meant to. That way we can keep bears in the wild woods, where they belong.

For Jack Carroll —A. R.

For Jean, who always helps me find my way home, and especially for Dad —M. H.

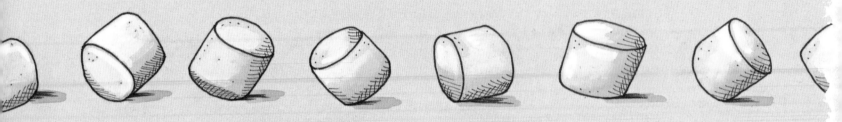

Text copyright © 2006 by Anne Rockwell
Illustrations copyright © 2006 by Megan Halsey

All rights reserved. No part of this book may be
reproduced or transmitted in any form or by any
means, electronic or mechanical, including photocopying,
recording, or by any information storage and retrieval
system, without permission in writing from the
publisher.

First published in the United States of America in
2006 by Walker Publishing Company, Inc.
Distributed to the trade by Holtzbrinck Publishers

For information about permission to reproduce
selections from this book, write to
Permissions, Walker & Company,
104 Fifth Avenue, New York, New York 10011

Library of Congress Cataloging-in-Publication Data

Rockwell, Anne F.
Backyard bear / Anne Rockwell ; illustrations by
Megan Halsey.
    p. cm.

ISBN-10: 0-8027-9573-0 (hardcover)
ISBN-13: 978-0-8027-9573-1 (hardcover)
ISBN-10: 0-8027-9574-9 (reinforced)
ISBN-13: 978-0-8027-9574-8 (reinforced)
1. Bears—Juvenile literature. 2. Urban animals—
Juvenile literature. I. Halsey, Megan, ill. II. Title.
QL737.C27R615 2006   599.78—dc22
2006000470

The illustrations for this book were created using pen
and ink and watercolor on toned watercolor paper.

Book design by Nicole Gastonguay

Visit Walker & Company's Web site at
www.walkeryoungreaders.com

Printed in China

10 9 8 7 6 5 4 3 2 1

All papers used by Walker & Company are natural, recyclable
products made from wood grown in well-managed forests.
The manufacturing processes conform to the environmental
regulations of the country of origin.